Η ΙΣΤΟΡΙΑ ΤΩΝ ΑΡΙΘΜΩΝ

THE NUMBER STORY

SMALL BOOK ONE

ENGLISH - GREEK

*Numbers Teach Children
Their Number Names*

written and illustrated by

MISS ANNA

Early Reader Edition of *The Number Story 1*
Bronze Medal Winner, 2016 Wishing Shelf Book Award

Library of Congress Control Number: 2018902040

Names: Miss Anna, author.
Title: Number story : numbers teach children their number names / Miss Anna.
Description: Portland, OR: Lumpy Publishing, 2018.
Identifiers: ISBN 978-1-945977-38-1 | LCCN 2018902040
Summary: The pictures and rhymes present stories which introduce numbers 0-10.
Subjects: LCSH Numeration—English--Greek--Pictorial works--Juvenile literature. | BISAC JUVENILE NONFICTION /
Languages: English--Greek
Classification: LCC QA141.3 .M57 2018 | DDC 513—dc23

Publisher: Lumpy Publishing
Website: www.missannabooks.com
Email: missanna@missannabooks.com

Paperback: ISBN 978-1-945977-38-1
Printed in the U.S.A.   1 3 5 7 9 10 8 6 4 2

Want to learn our number names?

Θέλεις να μάθεις τα ονόματα Αριθμούς μας;

It is very easy and a lot of fun!

Είναι πολύ εύκολο και έχει πολύ πλάκα!

Say-along our little jingle

Τραγουδήστε μαζί μας

starting from Number One!

Ξεκινώντας από το Νούμερο ένα!

1

ONE looks like my one finger.

α ★ ΕΝΑΣ

Μοιάζει με το ένα
μου δαχτυλάκι.

ONE!
ΕΝΑΣ!

2

TWO trails a tail.

β ΔΥΟ

Έχει μια ουρά.

A TAIL! MIA OYPA!

3

THREE   has bumps.

γ ☆ ΤΡΙΑ

Είναι σαν τους λόφους.

Κοιτάξτε τους λόφους!

4

FOUR   carries a sail.

δ ✶ ΤΕΣΣΕΡΑ

Έχει ένα πανί.

A SAIL!
Ένα Πανί!

5
FIVE   is a racing track.
ε ☆ ΠΕΝΤΕ
Είναι μια πίστα αγώνων.

VROOM
Βρουυυυυμ!
1

SIX   curves like a snail.

ς ☆ ΕΞΙ

Έχει μια καμπύλη
σαν σαλιγκάρι.

A SNAIL! Σαλιγκάρι!

7

SEVEN has a sharp angle.

ζ ΕΠΤΑ

Έχει μια κοφτερή γωνία.

OUCH!
ΑΟΥΤΣ!

8

EIGHT   is rollercoaster rails.

η ΟΚΤΩ

Είναι σαν ένα οδοστρωτήρα.

Γιούπιιι!
YIPPEE!

NINE   is a bubble on a stick.

θ ✦ ENNEA

Είναι μια φούσκα πάνω σε ραβδί.

A BUBBLE! Μια φούσκα!

TEN   is an eye of a whale.

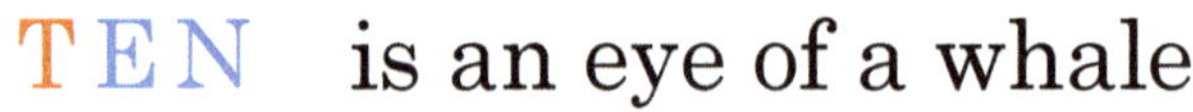

ι ΔΕΚΑ

Είναι το μάτι μιας φάλαινας.

HELLO!
Χαίρετε!

And
Και

0

ZERO   is an empty pail.

ΜΗΔΕΝ
Είναι ένα άδειο δοχείο.

IT'S
EMPTY!
Είναι Άδειο!

Thank you for playing with us today.

We had a lot of fun too!

Σε ευχαριστούμε που έπαιξες
μαζί μας σήμερα.

Περάσαμε και εμείς πολύ ωραία!

We are your Number friends,
Zero to Ten,
Who will be here for you~
Είμαστε οι φίλοι Αριθμοί σου,

Μηδέν μέχρι Δέκα.

Θα είμαστε εδώ για σένα~

Bye-bye now!
See you again soon!
Γειά σου τώρα!
Τα ξαναλέμε σύντομα!

The Numbers are *SINGING* too!

To sing-a-long, look for Miss Anna Number Story
at your favorite music store like iTUNES.

MP3

Numbers 0-10
IDENTIFYING & COUNTING

Numbers 11-20 & Ordinals
first, second, third...

Numbers 0-100 & Place Values
ones, tens, hundreds...

About Clocks & Telling Time
hours, minutes, seconds

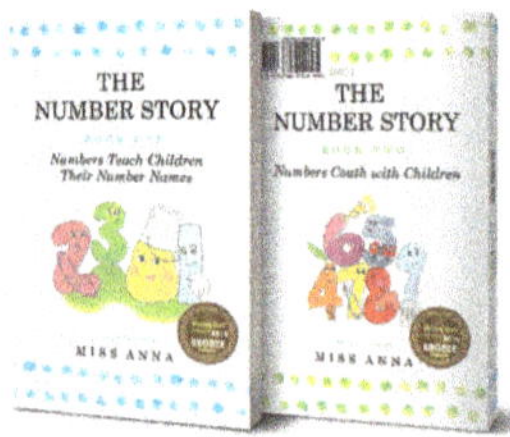

Number Story 1 & 2
isbn: 978-0-996216-48-7

Number Story 3 & 4
isbn: 978-1-945977-01-5

Number Story 5 & 6
isbn: 978-1-945977-06-0

Number Story 7 & 8
isbn: 978-1-949320-40-4

For more Miss Anna books to love,
visit us at

www.missannabooks.com

Numbers are working hard all over the world!
Come Travel the World with Us!

9 781945 977381